FIERCE FATTY

Love Your Body and Live Like the Queen You Already Are

Victoria Welsby
@bampowlife

For my father:

He lived, at times, being his brave authentic self (no matter how quirky it was), and at other times he couldn't.

"I learned that courage was not the absence of fear, but the triumph over it. The brave man is not he who does not feel afraid, but he who conquers that fear."

- NELSON MANDELA

TABLE OF CONTENTS

CHAPTER ONE:

INTRODUCTION

Hello, I am fat.

Fat is not my actual name – that would be weird, AND very cruel of my parents.

No, fat is the neutral word I use to describe my achingly fabulous body.

When I call myself fat, people rush to correct me "No, no! You're not fat! You're curvy, you're voluptuous, you're...fluffy."

I have been fat from as young as I can remember. Also from as young as I can remember, I have known that being fat is bad. Fat is the worst thing I can be, worse than someone who doesn't tip, worse than a kitten killer, worse than someone who doesn't signal while changing lanes!

Society teaches us being fat is bad. Fat discrimination is the fourth most prevalent form of discrimination. Our culture tells us repeatedly that the most desirable people are white, young and thin.

You can't "fix" the first two, but thin? Of course! Eat less, exercise more. Simple discipline, right?

It's not so simple though. The diet industry is so massive because it has repeat customers for life. But what if we spent less time, money and energy on the pursuit of thinness and instead focused on the things that actually matter? Like if pineapple on pizza should be outlawed, or if the mullet WAS the greatest haircut of the 20th Century. What if we lived in a society where every body type was not only accepted, but cherished?

Like me, you may find it so frustrating that the diet industry thrives on your failure. Half of everyone reading this book will go on a diet this year, telling yourself: *this time it'll be different, this time I'll get a bikini body, this time I'll transform my whole life...*

Last year Americans spent over $66 billion on trying to become thinner. 95% of diets fail and 1 in 3 dieters progress to pathological dieting.

You go on a diet, your diet fails, you think you're a greedy loser, and then you go back again for another round of punishment.

I did everything I could to get on the other side of that wall, the thin side, where gorgeous models danced in string bikinis, everyone was happy and money rained from the sky. With all my might I tried, but that wall was just too high, and I simply wasn't meant to scale it. The truth is that on the other side of the wall, everything is exactly the same as it is over here. We have been sold a timeshare in a space of land that we can never inhabit by a diet industry that profits on our desperate fear of being fat.

Had I known this fact, and learned to truly believe it at a young age, then my life would have been very different. Had I known that my worth wasn't measured by my dress-size, I would have realized that I was, and am, worthy. Had I known then that I was worthy, I wouldn't have dated creepy dudes, worked in jobs that I cried about on Sunday evenings, or lived an existence of "less than."

Now I know that I am a goddamned glorious queen and that I deserve the world, and I want to spread the gospel! I want every single person to know that they are worthy. YOU are worthy. You always were and you always will be.

Did you know that 9 out of 10 women are unhappy with their bodies (whereas 9 out of 10 men are happy with any woman's body. Am I right?). 89% of women cancel plans, job interviews and important life events simply because of how they look.

This is bananas, right?! We are not living our lives because we think our bodies don't measure up. And that, my friend, is bullshit!

So, how did I go from being a quivering meek pushover to a calm, confident, and resilient woman? Well, read on, hot stuff, and let me give you my brain changing recipe to living your life like the queen you really are.

CHAPTER TWO:

KNOW YOUR LESSONS

I haven't always been a rebel. Oh no, far from it, in fact.

My mother brought up four children on a part-time salary from working in a corner store. She was probably paid minimum wage, or not far from it. My mum detested her jobs and put up with abuse from her boss. My dad, was an alcoholic, didn't support the family and spent any money he got on drinking. He hated working so much that he stopped at the age of 40 and never went back. The way I saw it work was so extremely horrible and you'd have to sell your soul to make minimum wage.

This was one lesson I learned from my childhood, but not one that affected me in a dramatic way (although until my mid twenties I had jobs that would make me cry on a Sunday evening over, they were that bad).

But the other, more powerful lessons really stuck with me and shaped the way I viewed myself and participated in life. Not everything in my childhood sucked, there were magical times filled with love. I learned positive lessons about kindness, friendship and resiliency. Those lessons shaped me, too. But in this book we are trying to work out why at times we feel like a big bag of poo and an excellent place to start is from the very beginning. So, what lessons did I learn to help me believe I lacked worth?

Lesson One from the "You Are Not Worthy School": Your worth does not exceed that of a man's.

I had a father who put his own needs far above his family. He always told us that he didn't ever want kids, nor did he like them. My mother encouraged us to be as quiet as possible when my dad wasn't at the bar for fear of annoying him and making him mad.

My dad once got an insurance pay out from breaking his arm at work (in the short time in life he did have a job) and instead of using the money to help feed the family or buy any of the basic things we desperately needed to live, he instead took himself on a foreign holiday to watch Formula One car racing, by himself.

I cannot fathom being married to a man would take himself off for an exotic holiday when my mum barely had enough money to feed the family. Things like this didn't cause my mum to walk away however. I saw this type of behaviour as acceptable and understood that men get special treatment in life because they are just better people.

We lived in a dangerous neighbourhood and one time we got locked out of the house on a cold and rainy night. My mum went to a friends place to call my dad to ask him to come home to open the door. He refused and my mum had to leave us in our rickety car that was broken down, walk in the rain through unsafe streets to get his key. This was totally normal behaviour. He would never go out of his way to help his wife or his young children.

Lesson Two: Make yourself small and invisible to be safe.

One time I was invited to a birthday party at Burger King (and actually the only time I went to a fast food restaurant party), which was the best thing ever, of course. I came home with a balloon on a stick, #childhooddreamscomingtrue! I quietly played with it in the living room. Not quietly enough though, as my dad summoned me over, with his cigarette in one hand, and my balloon in the other hand, he brought the two together and promptly poppped it.

My dad couldn't stand the noise of children, and so when we got home from school we snuck by the living room where he sat watching his shows, drinking cider hoping he wouldn't notice us. On the days he was at the pub we would happily watch kids TV, but the moment we heard his moped coming through the back gate we switched the channel over to the shows he liked and made ourselves scarce.

Lesson Three: When people are mad they insult the worst thing about you; the way you look.

I really don't know how we afforded anything at all. My mom made things stretch as far as possible, watering down the milk, shopping in the cheapest places, taking multiple cleaning jobs. Because of this my mom was stressed and impatient.

"Victoria, you are such a lazy lump, move your fat arse!"

I was a good student, was quiet and obedient, but I saw that had a fatal flaw; being fat. I knew it was a terrible feature because it was the thing my mom mentioned when she was cross with me. And I didn't blame her, I was grotesque after all, she must have been so very embarrassed of me. Hindsight showed me these thoughts were wildly incorrect.

Luckily my dad would never be cruel to me about my appearance, apart from one time patting my wobbly thigh and telling me to go on a diet, only because my mum had put him up to it.

Lesson Four: Mom is fat, therefore you're a monster

This lesson came from the way my mom viewed herself. She described herself as the fat sister in her family. She was ugly, apparently. My mom is small, a petite lady, and so if she was fat, then that made me a monster!

There were many items of clothing in my mums closet that didn't fit, but she kept to slim down into. Items from decades before that didn't even fit my child body (even more proof that I was too big). The reality was that my mum had birthed six children in total and her body had changed from the time she was a teenager.

Her body had given life six times over, but that didn't make it miraculous, beautiful or strong. It made it lumpy, stretched, used. She never described herself as acceptable, never mind beautiful (which she was, and still is).

Lesson Five:
Observing my parents' relationship. My mom did everything for my dad and he was very controlling,

but it was the only relationship I saw. It was normal to wait hand and foot on your spouse, wasn't it? No matter what selfish acts he put her through wasn't enough to make her get a divorce until they'd spent multiple years together. Everyone was afraid of their dad, weren't they? One time I had dinner around a friends house and she spoke to her dad the same way she spoke to her mom, normally, playfully. I whispered to her "How can you speak to your dad like that? Won't he shout at you?" She was confused and laughed "Of course not."

Lesson Six: I am greedy

We were poor, and therefore we lived in food scarcity.

Every Sunday we would go to Kwik Save (the cheapest bargain supermarket), and buy that coming weeks food. I vividly remember that a real treat was the corned beef from the deli counter- it tasted so goddamn delicious mixed with ketchup that it would be gone before the day was out. I remember that bloody corned beef so well, because we lived deprived of food and so, I naturally started to fixate on food. I desired it so much that I would sneak food when no one was looking. My desire for food was so feverish that I felt incredibly out of control... and wildly greedy.

In our house, it was a very special day when we got any cereal but value Cornflakes, but for some reason, on this very special morning we had Coco Pops in the house. I remember gleefully having a bowl, feeling unbelievable joy. I wanted another bowl, of course. I asked my mum, she said no, I begged her "Please!" I don't know her reasons, but I can guess it was stress, having no money, having 3 other kids who would want a bowl of Coco Pops, having a chubby kid harassing her for more of this expensive treat... but her reaction was to slap me across the face and shut me in the kitchen. "Here, eat them all!" I sat on the cold kitchen floor crying, pouring myself another bowl, knowing that I would be comforted with every bite. When my mum turned her back on me, her slovenly, greedy, out of control daughter, I thought, "At least I have food".

The reality was that my glorious body was doing everything it could to make me want food because I didn't have it in abundance. I didn't know that whenever I was hungry I could open a cupboard and have my fill of anything I desired. The delirious feelings I got from food (which were signals my body were giving me as a reward for getting food) made me fixate on it. This euphoric reaction I had, made food so lovely, so giving, and so, so special to me. To compound the effects from food scarcity, was having a sibling with bulimia. I was trained to grab the food I wanted as quickly as possible because if I didn't it would be gone, and also, wouldn't be replaced. Looking back, I now know that impulse was caused by one birthday. When I came home after being out with friends, to find that all of my birthday dinner had been eaten, along with my birthday cake.

So with these core lessons I learned about myself, I knew that I was fat, which equalled ugly. Because I was ugly, I should be lucky that anyone would consider being with me; I *was* hideous after all. I should be grateful for any attention. From those core lessons I learned that life was hard, I would hate my job, because doesn't everyone hate their job? I would not be fulfilled, *could* not be fulfilled. I learned that I shouldn't expect much from my spouse, because I actually didn't deserve to have anyone more than a shade above abusive. And finally, I learned that I shouldn't take up space, don't speak up, others are more important.

My childhood experience isn't unique. Many people experience a lot worse and take different lessons away with them. My parents weren't evil, they were simply doing the best that they could at the time. And sometimes they *weren't* trying their best. They made mistakes; as complex human beings, we all make mistakes. Unfortunately, my young experiences molded me into a meek, subservient young woman who was eager to please.

What experiences from your childhood or your young adult life have shaped the way you view yourself? Think about the lessons you were continually taught, the messages you absorbed. Did you feel loved wholly and unconditionally or was there another story at play that could've hurt your self-esteem?

So you can imagine from the perception I had about myself, it was no surprise that when I was 17 I met a 30 year old alcoholic who lived with his mother, and I thought he was a real catch!

How did I get to being with a mega loser at 17? Well, when I was 16 my mom decided she should move back to Ireland where she is from. I convinced her that I was old enough, and wise enough to stay behind. I wanted to finish my last year of school, so just after my 17th birthday, my mom left and sold the family home.

What I didn't know is that you had to be 18 to rent a place, and my salary as a part time cleaner after school wouldn't stretch to paying rent. I was just too young to understand how to look after myself. I didn't even know how to wash my clothes, cook or any other "adult" responsibilities. So I ended up homeless. I lived in a shelter for young people and I told hardly anyone my predicament. I went to school as normal and pretended everything was okay. Really, I wasn't *that* worried. I mean, did *I* really deserve a safe home? Even when residents broke into the shower while I was naked, trying to humiliate me. Even when another teenager was screaming wildly outside where I slept, trying to get in. Even when I was terrified.

I truly believed I wasn't worth more.

When a creepy 30-year-old bought me a lollipop (*shudder*) and said I was pretty, I was in heaven! He rescued me from the homeless shelter, moving me in with his elderly mother and four cats. We saw each other every day from the time we met and I thought he was so handsome and wonderful. Now, looking back I'm like, "Girl, NOOOOO!," but with a self-esteem as low as mine was, I couldn't see the red flags, and even if I did, I ignored them. After all I was lucky to even have a boyfriend!

I was with him for two years and in that time he wore down the tiny flicker of light I had in my belly. The tiny light that told me that maybe, *maybe*, I did deserve more. He was abusive, controlling and dangerous. It took him chasing me through the streets with a knife before I had the courage to leave. He wouldn't let me leave, of course. He stalked me and my family members until I got a restraining order against him. He threw a brick through my window, punched my boss, went to my sister's work. Eventually he gave up, but even though I was physically safe, the mental scars would take years to heal.

When people say, "I don't understand why they just doesn't leave!" about abusive relationships,

I understand their misplaced frustrations. I also understand how some people feel about themselves to end up with partners like I did. I understand how leaving seems like an impossible and very risky feat. It's like saying to a passenger aboard a hijacked plane "just leave!" It's not that simple. Abusive partners hijack your life, and hold you hostage.

I was broken. I was a victim. I blamed others.

But I had a solution to fix everything...lose weight!

The abusive guy had put me on a diet and it had worked. I say diet, but what I mean is that he starved and controlled me, while monitoring what I ate. When I say it "worked", I mean that it gave me some serious disordered eating patterns, temporary weight loss and eventual weight gain.

Naturally, losing weight this time would bring me everything I could dream of, right? It was because I was fat that I attracted loser guys. It was because I was so ugly that I had crappy jobs. If only I was thin, I would spend my life on tropical beaches, sipping cocktails as hunky shirtless men fanned me with palm leaves.

I eagerly started going to weekly weigh-ins, counting points and reading diet magazines. With every pound I lost, I knew I was one step closer to being worthy. I dreamed about getting to my goal weight and bumping into old friends, revelling in their praise and envy.

I began to feel self-righteous about the fatties who weren't on diets. If they weren't so *lazy* and just *tried,* then they could be on the journey to becoming thin just like me! All they had to do was eat...well, close to nothing and exercise excessively, and keep that up for the rest of their lives. And anyway, this wasn't a diet. This was a lifestyle change (LOL). I was swapping my old fat, sad loser life for a life of spandex, fabulousness, sugar-free, fat-free dust eating.

What I didn't know then was that I was doomed to fail. 95% of dieters are. Even when I did starve my way to a "straight size" body, I didn't get the things I dreamed of. Not even close. At my very thinnest, I still felt too big, I still wasn't confident, I still dated creeps, and I still hated my job. I was still too scared to leave my hometown. I was just the same old Victoria with the same old problems, but with a smaller body.

As a child I had learnt false lessons about my worth. That wasn't my fault. However, as a young adult I chose to keep using these lessons to keep me in victim mode. What I didn't realize was that as an adult I had a choice to use that pain as a catalyst for change, instead I just used it as an excuse to play small, while feeling way too big.

I focused on losing weight, when in reality I should have focused on losing the emotional baggage that was the actual thing that was weighing me down.

A couple of years later I'm in my local bar. You know the type of place. Reeks of vomit and your shoes stick to the floor. Maybe you've seen a girl like me, afraid to say no. What if I never get propositioned again? And anyway, I'm lucky he'd even consider me.

That's how I got my next boyfriend, Dan. Tall, green eyes, a smooth talker who screamed of trouble with a capital T. But I was smitten. Have you ever been so in love that you knew you would be together forever? He worshipped me, or so I thought, and talked about making me his wife. He could do no wrong! A man that wanted to marry me?! Maybe there was hope after all. An idea! I'm going to make Dan love me even more with a dream vacation. Bed and Breakfast, on the beach. Spain at sunset. Smitten, he'll fall to one knee.

And if I stay on my current diet, maybe I'll be thin enough to wear a bikini. That would be a first!

So a week later, I'm in his bedroom, waiting for Dan, sprawled out on the bed in my sexiest underwear with two plane tickets, when I hear a key in the lock, the door opening and Dan's footsteps as he approaches the bedroom.

Only, it's not Dan. It's a woman.

"Who are you!?" I scream.

"Sarah. Dan's girlfriend, who are you?"

"Victoria. Dan's girlfriend!" This must be the "psycho ex" he was telling me about.

But then she shows me her hair dryer that Dan said he bought for me, and her toothbrush she uses when she stays over, that Dan also said he bought for me!

You may know the feeling; like a bomb exploding, my ears are ringing, there's chaos everywhere. Total disbelief. I grabbed my sexy underwear and bunny slippers that Sarah probably thinks Dan bought for her, and drove away in a daze.

I'm still too fat to keep a man interested. No wonder he cheated. My job is awful, I hate where I live, I hate myself. This body has always been a disappointment. What has it given me in return, extra warmth in the winter and increased buoyancy? It's not enough.

There were four of us that he was cheating on and with. All three of the other women were thinner than me.

I cannot survive this, the pain is just too much!

So, I go to a place I feel unconditional love. The potato chip aisle at Safeway.

I was in heaven. Mmm, those salty Pringles made me feel something a man never had. I feverishly turned my attention to my other beau: milk chocolate. OMG you smooth, sweet Prince, come to mama. I danced through the bread aisle, embracing steamy baguettes as Skittles rained from the sky, coating me in sugary kisses.

But by the time I reached the checkout line, I felt empty. Despite being anything but. Alone. Foolish. Unwanted. Then a magazine caught my eye: a cover celebrating Paralympians who overcame impossible odds. The one beside it – an 80-year-old woman who invented a dating app for seniors.

Finally I saw the most shocking cover of all.

Bold horizontal stripes on a fat Cover Girl?! And it wasn't a diet magazine with a story about how she lost 5000 lbs in 3 minutes. She was not even embarrassed about being fat, in fact, she liked it?!

No fucking way.

CHAPTER THREE:

CHANGE YOUR NEURAL PATHWAYS

For years, before I embraced this goooorgeous body, I tried everything I could to trick people into not noticing I am fat, hoping that they would see me and think, "Wow, is that a British Tyra Banks?"

I would do things like buy clothes in sizes too small for me in case my label would stick out and people would see that it was a medium instead of the XXL it should have been. I would wear shape underwear that was so tight that I would lose the ability to speak for the duration of wearing them. I would dazzle people with my incredible personality, blinding them with jokes so that they wouldn't notice my fatness. Then I was exposed to an image of a fat woman whose attitude was "I am fucking fabulous, and if you don't like it, suck it."

This was a brand new concept, never one I'd seen or considered before.

How could anyone be happy to be fat? Fat meant ugly, unworthy, unhealthy, embarrassing...didn't it? Back at home from the supermarket, the magazine was open on my lap. The plus-sized model was saying: "Tired of self-hate? Become a sassy fat badass. Be a rebel. Build a new tribe!"

And she had some advice: Get rid of toxic people. Start with your social media.

I opened my Facebook.

Weird Uncle Keith continually ranting about Millennials. Unfollow. Schoolmate Michelle "I'm on the Brazilian Bikini Belly Bootcamp Diet." God, she's already 100 lbs smaller than me!" Unfollow. My vegan friend who keeps declaring her undying love for lettuce and dust and she calls herself a foodie. At least commit to it, like I have! In fact, all vegans, unfollow!

We spend hours every day engaging with social media online. It makes total sense that we are influenced by what we continually consume. When my Instagram feed was filled with fitness gurus and skinny girl eating plans, subconsciously I learned that I didn't measure up. I learned that the most desirable was white, young, able-bodied and thin. Our brains are magical and help us with thinking quickly and automatically.

Remember a time when you learned something new, let's say riding a bike. To begin with it was really hard, and you'd fall off, cycle into bushes and think this two-wheel contraption was out to end your life! But after a while you got a hang of it, and before long it was second nature.

Now when you hop on a bike, you barely have to think about it. The reason for this is because through repetition you created a neural pathway in your brain. A "road" in your noggin where thoughts can whiz through at lightning speed, so you no longer have to *think* about riding your bike.

Neural pathways mean that we are not constantly having to make decisions, or learn and can get on with more important brain activities... Like if you'd rather play tonsil hockey with Channing Tatum or Hugh Jackman... or maybe both together?

So when you are on social media you are "riding your bike" with the images you are consuming. Facebook filled with complaining, racist relatives? Instagram a wall of goal bodies and diet inspiration? Pinterest a sea of Photoshopped yogis in seemingly impossible poses? You are teaching your brain that this is what is desirable, this is what you should look like, this is who you should be.

And that simply isn't possible for us to achieve. 5% of women have that "ideal" physique that we are told is the most desirable, and when that 5% is shown online, their bodies are often edited, manipulated and have a glowy filter making them look even more dreamy... and unattainable.

When we look at our own bodies in the mirror we just don't look like these images that we see day in and day out. Neural pathways are being created in our brains telling us that this is what it is to be appealing. It's no wonder when we see "flaws" we struggle to love them! It's incredibly frustrating to me that I spent so long trying, desperately, to just move the needle closer towards looking like unrealistic representations of women. If only I knew that I was already a fucking queen!

Once I changed the images I was consuming daily, I began creating new neural pathways in my magnificent brain. It took time however. I began finding images of plus-size models, following clothing companies that catered to fat babes. Then I found other fierce fatties, influencers, business women, activists, mums, burlesque stars... All with incredible and diverse body types.

One day I was doing some online shopping, looking at some cute plus-size dresses. I clicked onto a new page and a page of images of straight size models came up. Initially I didn't recognise what I was looking at. I just noticed that they looked different and I couldn't put my finger on why. They seemed different from the "norm."

That's when I realized that I had stumbled upon the straight size section and for a moment my brain was not used to the images. My neural pathway was no longer so deeply entrenched into thinking "this is what you should look like." That's when I knew my brain had done some incredible hard work making some juicy new neural pathways. And my new neural pathways saw beauty in a vast range of body types. When I see a straight sized model, I no longer automatically covet her Photoshopped body. I just observe, notice what feelings I have, or not think much at all!

That was the beginning of finding my new rebel self. It all starts with one small step. And my first step was a seeing a fat woman who knew she was a queen, and then a simple unfollow on Facebook. The new rebel self however was still a sapling at the confidence and body acceptance game. I was at the start of the journey and still had a lot of work to do. That work involved becoming "battle ready" for the real world that I had to live in. I wasn't a Confidence Warrior just yet.

CHAPTER FOUR:

BE BRAVE
(even if you're shitting your pants with fear)

I continued to surround myself with positive people, and I discovered that there is a whole movement of people who are striving to love their bodies unconditionally - hundreds, actually, there are thousands of them in fact!

And one day, scrolling through Instagram I see a post that says, "What would you do if you had no fear?" In my case, it was, "what would you do if you weren't wasting your time dieting?"

My first list was pretty short:

One

I wouldn't wait to become a certified supermodel before looking for a new job, I would seek rewarding work now.

Two

Take that vacation to Spain, wear a swimsuit on the beach and maybe find me an oiled Will Smith look alike. (Honestly, that's the first thing I did and second and third and...well, you get the picture).

Three

If I wasn't wasting my life dieting, I would finally love myself...unconditionally.

I did the first two things. I even posted a picture of myself in my bikini online! But loving myself... that was SO hard.

That small flash of bravery led me to taking other small steps. The courage you feel doesn't need to be long-lasting or genuine. It doesn't matter where the motivation for courage comes from, you just have to use that emotion to push yourself forward.

If I could fly to a different country, then maybe I could go to that Beyoncé dance class. If I could go to a Beyoncé dance class, maybe I could have a life I loved...maybe.

Fear is a real doozy to overcome, it's one hell of powerful emotion, and for good reason! If we didn't feel fear, then we would literally be dead. We'd all be like "I'mma ride this roller coaster with no seatbelt, bitches" or "I love meeting dudes off Craigslist in that creepy back alley late at night, he said he just wants to cuddle!"

Honor the fact that fear is a motherfucker and realize, it's going to take itty bitty steps (and sometimes humongous leaps) to overcome it.

I view any big goal or scary task that I need to do like a cake. If someone put a giant chocolate cake in front of you and said "Eat it all!" you could have a go at it. It would be overwhelming though. After the first few slices you start getting full, by the fourth you'd feel unmotivated, and by the sixth, you'd be swearing off sponge based desserts for the rest of your life.

That's what we normally do when we try to tackle fear; we try to eat the whole cake. When we aren't successful, we swear off "cake eating" and try to avoid attempting the ordeal again.

The method I use is to come up with a realistic plan so that I know I can succeed. I plan by taking just one teeny tiny slice of the cake, and then seeing how that feels, how it tastes. Do I like this? Do I want to keep doing this? If your goal is, for example, to find a delicious person to date, but the idea of actually dating makes you want to vomit in your mouth, then you'd want to start small. So the first slice of cake for you could be writing down a list of qualities you'd look for in a significant other. Then you may want to take a bigger slice of cake; say take some sweet pictures of yourself for your dating profile and writing a bio.

At any point if it feels too much, you can go back to taking smaller slices, or take a breather. The more cake you eat, the more confident you'll be in your cake eating abilities.

Whatever fear or goal you have may mean it could take longer to achieve. Some fears may be giant 20 tier wedding cakes, and so break that shit down into small mouthfuls, or start on a smaller cake to begin with.

What "mouthful" can you take right now? What "slice" can you serve yourself?

I promise you'll start feeling stronger and more capable once you start taking small steps. You'll also start to realize that you have this Confidence Warrior lurking inside bursting to come out.

I was starting to build my courage muscles, and beginning to feel brave. I started to realize that I was worth more, in every aspect of my life. So one day, I asked for a meeting with my boss. Calmly, but still with a little hesitation, I questioned "Can I have a pay raise? I was thinking of a 2K bump." He stopped me dead. "Victoria, you are not worth 2K more!" In that moment, listening to him explain to me why I wasn't worth a pay raise and, in fact I should be lucky that I had a job at all (!!!), I realized I wasn't internalizing his opinions about me. There was this defiant voice that said, "Girl, you're worth a million bucks!"

My boss was right, I wasn't worth a 2K pay raise. I was worth a 12K pay raise, which is what I got at the new job I secured just weeks later. Because I had taken smaller steps in my life, the bigger ones weren't such a massive deal anymore.

I realized that I had made external changes, but internally I still truly believed I didn't measure up because I was fat. That had to change! So from here, every time a doubt popped into my head about my success, I questioned it. "Is it true you're going to be fired tomorrow, or is that thought coming from insecurity?" "Do you really look like a sweaty pig/whale hybrid in that outfit, or do you look achingly fabulous?"

There were so many of these thoughts coming up daily, and often I would just agree with them. "YES! I do look like a sweaty pig/whale hybrid today!" Slowly, I began catching more of them and my internal dialogue went from meek to sassy.

"You *are* worthy! You always were and you always will be!"

Eventually, I was able to analyze negative thoughts, understand where they were coming from and show myself compassion. You know how people say "treat yourself like you would your best friend," well that was too hard for me, so instead my goal was to treat myself the way I would an animal. Think about it if your cat has a big fluffy belly you're like "OMG, why are you so adorable?!" If your dog gets into something he shouldn't, while telling him off, you're secretly thinking what a lovable rascal he is.

New mission: treat yourself like a goddamn animal!

So, I've done all these brave things. But, I'm still fat. I am still wearing my shame on my body. Everyone can see I'm a fraud and a failure. If I *really* had my life together, I would be thin, right?

One day, scrolling through Instagram again I see a post that says, "It's okay to be fat." A concept I had heard before, but had not yet really believed.

The poster clearly misunderstood what it meant to be successful. At the time, I scoffed at the idea, but let it sit with me. Slowly those words sank in. "What if it's okay to be fat?" Yeah, what if it *was* okay to be fat? What if this perceived flaw I had wasn't a flaw at all? What if I was okay all along? What if I was worthy, then, now and in the future, no matter what?

CHAPTER FIVE:

DO IT FOR THE CHILDREN
(and your future)

I remember going shopping with my mom for a school uniform. I am standing in the changing room with the unforgiving lights glaring down on me, trying with all my might to fit into the biggest children's shirt in the store. The buttons are bulging at the seams and no amount of sucking in my stomach can hide the fact that my body is just too big. My mom, being frustrated and wanting to know what was taking so long, pulls the curtain open. There I am for her to see. Her mortified daughter, whose body didn't fit.

"Victoria! How can you be too fat for the biggest size?"

At that moment I realised I had to overcome this fatal flaw. I vowed to become better, become thinner, and become worthy, and as a child I tried many things to get there.

I didn't eat lunch at school, instead hiding in the library reading books. I sprinted up and down the corridors counting in one hundred lap intervals. I had this wild idea that eating bland food would make me thinner. "The worse it tastes, the less on my waist!" I prayed, "God, give me the willpower to become anorexic." I just wanted the desire to stop eating.

All this before the age of 11. Did you know 46% of 9-11 year olds diet, and 91% of college women try to control their weight through restrictive eating?

People with larger bodies are more likely to be convicted of crimes, are systematically paid less, are punished harsher by their parents as children and will receive subpar medical treatment. All because they have bodies that are bigger.

Some people think, "But Victoria, this idea of being nice to fatties is a good idea and all, but what about the fact that fat people are unhealthy and they sit at home eating donuts off their fingers like rings?"

To them I say: What if I told you that you can be fat and healthy and on the other hand, thin and unhealthy? You can also be thin and healthy and fat and unhealthy.

Our weight doesn't determine our health status.

And even if it did, and you are unhealthy, you are still worthy as a human being. Bottom line, no matter what you look like, fat, thin, tall, short, mullet sporting or pineapple on pizza eating, you are worthy as a human being.

If only society could accept that humans come in many different varieties, it would've saved so many children learning that they are not enough – lessons they get from their parents, from society, from media.

So why is this? Why do we have a preference for thin? And not just a preference for thinness, but thin, white, young and able-bodied? Is this just a Western epidemic?

Let me tell you a story.

In 1995, the people of Fiji did not have television, as it had not been introduced yet. Another thing Fijians didn't have were eating disorders. There was not a single case of an eating disorder at all. Three years after TV arrived, 30% of Fijian school girls had developed high eating disorder symptoms. The rate of bulimia went from 0% to 11%.

The children who watched more television were 50% more likely to describe themselves as being "too big or fat."

So basically put, we created this preference. Our society, our culture, and the media we produce and consume tells us what is desirable. Which is good! Because it means that we can change it. We have the power to change the stories for all of the children out there who think they're not enough, or are too much.

I wanted to know why we still have this deep rooted aversion to fatness, so I started doing some of my own research about people's opinions of fat bodies.

I surveyed over a hundred Canadians and asked them what their ideal body type was. "Athletic" and "average" made up 60% of the vote. The least desired body type by far was "fat."

31% of respondents said the world would be a better place if there were less fat people in it. One third of the people who pass me on the street think the world would be better if I were either not here, or if there were less of me. And not just me, but they would like there to be 67% less of the world's population; for that is how many of us are plus-size.

The overarching theme was "It's fine if someone else wants to be fat, but not me, no thank you!" I was told that they would rather work with their archenemy, be publically humiliated or have people think they're a bad person rather than be fat.

The reason why is that they feared that fatness came with an automatic death sentence, being fat meant you would no longer be able to experience life in the fullest way possible.

The truth is, however, that being fat doesn't automatically mean you don't exercise, it doesn't mean you can't have a wonderful career, happy life, or deep and meaningful relationships; it doesn't mean you're unlovable or unworthy.

I discovered something on this journey: a change of public perception starts with the change of your own perception.

Only once you realize that you can do anything you want, and being a dress size bigger won't actually change that fact, will society-at-large realize that people who are large are just like me, and you.

You loving and accepting yourself unashamedly is a political act. You are literally changing the world for those who come after you and those who surround you.

Be the change you want to be. Use this power you harness as the motivation you may need when times are tough and you feel overwhelmed. Don't doubt the impact you can have on this world with simple changes in your perception.

Author's Note: You can read all of the survey responses at the back of this book.

CHAPTER SIX

BE SASSY AND BADASSY
(AKA Know Your Worth)

I love being surrounded by fierce fatties.

And I start going to the extreme. I built a website eager to share my life-changing experiences with everyone. I get supportive comments from people all over the world, but not everyone is pleased with my new-found confidence.

My email pings with a new message: "You are disgusting, fat people are unhealthy and pathetic."

Fat people aren't at home guzzling lard milkshakes 24 hours a day, contrary to some people's beliefs. But of course, you don't need to be healthy to be a worthy human being.

Another message: "I'm sorry but fat people can't dance and should be covered from head to toe as a courtesy to humanity. Go back to the sea, you whale."

You could be right, but you never know, one day you may just see a bikini clad dancing whale.

And finally a troll who has a heartwarming wish: "Fatphobia kills people? Only in my dreams." (Fatphobia which in case you're not familiar with the word, is the fear, or dislike of fat or fat people).

My crime? Living in a fat body without shame.

Thanks to these trolls, and many more, I finally worked out that I don't need to be thin to be worthy.

The thing is when a fat woman thinks she is fabulous or even if she thinks she is just alright, some people can get a little hot under the collar. Behind the anonymity of the internet my comments section can get...interesting.

Luckily I can see these comments for what they are: misguided, sad, cloaked in misogyny, classism and pain. Someone who is content with their lot in life is not spending their time writing cruel messages on the internet. And so I give them no power, because truly that's what they hold. In fact, I now believe that every nasty message represents two people who I have helped, and so the more hate, the more impact I am making in the world! So bring on the trolls! And what a better way to remind me that there is still so much work to do. If everyone agreed with my message, then I wouldn't have the power to change the world. We *all* have the power to change the world by living in our bodies, unashamed.

Apart from online criticism, you may find that those in your real life are "concerned" about you loving yourself. So I have created a list of sassy, badassy ways to respond when people are throwing shade about your appearance, your food choices, your lifestyle decisions. Of course, you don't have to say anything to anyone, but if you want to, take a little sass from here.

If someone says "You're fat!":

I know, thanks for noticing, don't I look GORGEOUS!

Oh wow! I am so glad to meet my own personal dietitian. Please tell me more about the nutritional value of kale?

I'm so sorry you have to degrade people to feel better about yourself.

It's interesting how you think it's appropriate to comment on my body.

Do other people know you're this rude?

With the "are you pregnant" question: YES! I had Mexican for lunch so I am expecting the arrival of a healthy 10 lb burrito sometime this afternoon!

Did you really just say that? Like, really?!

I am SO PROUD to be fat and fierce, baby!

If someone says "You should do this/ don't do that":

Raise hand to your eyebrow pretending to look for something in the distance and say "I'm sorry I was just looking for who actually asked you for your opinion."

It's cool how you think you know more about my life than I do. Please, do continue.

Remember when I asked for your opinion? No, me either.

If I wanted to hear from an ass, I'd fart.

I'm not interested in listening to people's opinions right now.

I only listen to advice from people who pay my bills. You don't pay me. You don't get a say.

Why do you think it's appropriate to tell me what to do?

If someone says, "I am concerned about your health," then say "If you were really concerned about my health, you'd be concerned about my mental health too."

Person says "OMG, have you lost weight?!":

Change the subject totally. "Nice weather today."

Oh sweet baby Jesus, I hope not!

No, but I look GOOD don't I?! You know, it's probably all this happiness from not dieting.

No.

Wow, do you monitor my body weight a lot? It must get tiring keeping tabs on me like that!

I'm too busy being fabulous to notice my weight.

Do you think it's appropriate to comment on someone's body?

Not if I can help it!

Is weight loss something that's important to you because it's not to me.

Or the one you can use in any situation:

Go fuck yourself.

Or the one if you're trying to have a genuine conversation:

Hey, I'm trying to work on loving my body and so can you try to avoid talking about weight/dieting/fat as a negative?

One of the big lines that fatphobic bigots like to say is "But what about your health?! All the diabetes, cancer, heart disease you're spreading." If I could eye roll any harder, I'd see the back of my neck. Fatphobes don't care about your health. If they did, then they wouldn't be fatphobic! They would understand that shaming folks is counterproductive (it literally makes people fatter) and simply a dick move. Being fat does not cause all of these scary diseases. Correlation is not causation. Being fat isn't something that people can catch. There is no such thing as the "obesity epidemic."

We are fed such fatphobic bullshit from all corners of our life and culture, it's hard to separate fact from fiction. If being healthful is something you want to pursue, then that's good for you. Also, if being healthful is something that doesn't interest you, then that is also good for you. Neither choice is more morally superior and you do not owe health to anyone. Also, being healthy is not something everyone *can* attain. If you do want to pursue a healthful lifestyle, or continue with the healthful lifestyle you already lead, but don't know how to track that without tracking your weight, then consider other indicators:

Can you move your body in the ways you want to? If not, then get a pole and start practicing your high kicks and back bends with flair while shaking your tatas like a Polaroid picture...or whatever floats your boat.

Do you feel good in your body? Work out how to feel better without focusing on weight. How about practicing self-care, building strength, giving your body yummy foods to make it happy, working on your mental health, having a glorious nap, binge watching the new hit Netflix show and not leaving your house for two days?

There's a meme out there that reads:

> Patient: "Doctor, help! I've been impaled on a stake!"
> Doctor: "Well, have you tried losing weight?"

It astounds me how weight loss is so often prescribed for no reason. When weight loss, as we know, doesn't work, makes people sick and causes folks to be fatter in the long run. News flash; there is no such thing as a healthy weight as health and weight are not correlated. Health is a construct and valuing healthy bodies is ableist. Saying that, not all doctors have the same attitude towards us fatties. There are lots of service providers that work with the Health At Every Size (HAES) model, which is so goddamn glorious. There are tons of resources on the HAES website (www. haescommunity.com) including lists of people who practice HAES professionally in different capacities.

Health at Every Size is a movement that celebrates all body types, challenges scientific and cultural assumptions about bodies and basically supports the idea that you can be, well, healthy at any size. Criticisms of the movement include that HAES can value health very heavily, so watch out for that.

CHAPTER SEVEN

STOP DIETING

So what if you want to get off the diet roller coaster for good? It can be tough for many reasons, but let me tell you how.

You are living in a society that tells you what to find attractive, tells you what beauty is. Right now beautiful is seen as thin, white and young, long legged, eyebrows shaped for the gods, flowing hair, thigh gapped...you get the picture. If you don't fall into those categories, tough luck, *you're ugly girl.* But that's okay, you can try to get those characteristics, right?

Or can you? And at what cost.

Let's break down the thin category. It's one of the most pervasive beauty ideals and is a real money spinner for the diet industry. That same diet industry last year was worth 66 billion dollars.

You want to look gorgeous so you go on a diet, because thin equals gorgeous (or so society tells us). You join Weight Watchers or sign up for some hot new juice cleanse. Everything feels hopeful and exciting. You lose weight quickly, the diet works! Why didn't you do this earlier? You feel great! Soon enough though, the sparkle dulls. The weight loss slows down, even though you're still eating a meager amount of food and exercising loads. Eventually you throw the towel in and not long after that, you put on the weight you lost...and often more.

You're back where you started, feeling terrible about yourself, but it's even worse because you weigh more and if you were only better, more dedicated you would've maintained the weight loss and finally be thin. You would finally be gorgeous. So you start again, this time on a new diet that will *really* work. But, it doesn't, because 95% of all diets fail.

That's the diet roller coaster of hell and millions of women are stuck on it and cannot get off. Some don't even realize that this roller coaster sucks balls and will continue riding it for the remainder of their lives. Okay, so let's lay some ground work here before I tell you *how* to get off the diet roller coaster by dispelling some super common and harmful myths we all hear every day.

Myth One: Fat Equals Death

Numerous studies have shown that weight and health are not correlated. In fact, <u>those who are "overweight"* live longer than those who are "underweight" and even a "normal" weight</u>. The amount of fat on your body does not equate to how long you'll live, what diseases you'll get and your health status. This is so hard to get your head around this though because companies, governments, your family, your annoying Aunt Gertrude all tell us that being fat is worse than being a kitten killer.

The thing is happy and healthy fat people don't make companies money.

And even if you are thin, there are other things the beauty industry will go after to make you feel insecure (i.e. all the beauty ideals listed above).

Myth Two: Anyone can lose weight, my Uncle Barry did, so you should too!

As we know, 95% of diets fail. And to be "successful" weight loss can be as little as a few pounds, and on top of that, studies fail to follow the 5% longer than two years. On top of *that* a massive portion of the 95% end up putting on more weight than they started with. So Uncle Barry lost 10lbs on a diet last year, but what you don't know is that he put back on 15.

Myth Three: You just need willpower!

"People who can't lose weight just lack willpower and are greedy"...yeah, not so much. Fat people actually consume *less* calories than their thin counterparts because being on the diet roller coaster messes with your metabolism. Just check out the heartbreaking stats from the contestants, ahem victims, on The Biggest Loser.

Your body is so remarkable and looks after you all own its own. All it asks from you is to feed and water it, keep it warm and let it sleep. But we have to mess with it and try to override our natural instincts. When we go on a diet our bodies think we are in a famine, and we *are*, a forced starvation. So what it does is magic; it holds onto the calories we *do* consume. It makes us desire calorie dense food; in fact, it makes us fixate on food and crave it like never before. Our body does everything it can to sabotage our efforts and help us "survive." That's why when you lose weight quickly on a diet and then plateau, it's our bodies taking over and trying to stabilize our weight.

Then guess what our incredible bodies do? They increase our set point weight (a 10-20lb weight range our bodies prefer to be at) so that we are safer in case another "famine" comes along. It also lowers our metabolic rate so that now we have to eat less to maintain our weights. Our bodies are protecting us from these unstable environments. It's a wonderful thing really, but totally the opposite effect people are trying to go for.

We are bombarded from every angle with meal plans and food pyramids that we don't need, so we end up not trusting our bodies when they say "feed me, please, for the love of baby Jesus!" Your body is so smart. Let it do its thing. It knows what it wants to eat, what nutrients it craves, when it's hungry and when it's full.

Myth Four: Just eat "good" food and avoid "bad" food

Little known fact: there were actually 11 Commandments, not 10! Yeah for some reason number 11 was lost through history, but is indelibly marked on the brains of every good citizen of the world: "Thou shall not eat foods that are delicious, for these foods are bad and you shall repent your sins by eating food that you dislike, but is morally pure."

Yeah, so there is morally "good" and morally "bad" foods! Who knew? Well apart from every single diet roller coaster rider out there. Now, this may come as a surprise to you, but food is just...food. Just something to nourish your brain or your body, or even both! You are not a bad person for eating a whole extra-large pizza from Domino's. In fact, in my eyes, I think that makes you pretty badass!

You can use food in any way you wish, it's *your* choice.

You may have to deal with people who don't yet know this fact, however, and say things like "Do you really need to eat that?" or "Did you know that donuts have like a million calories?" This is one of the hazards of getting off the diet roller coaster, but fear not, you will soon be strong and sassy enough to tell these bozos to relax to the max (they are probably on the roller coaster too and not having a fun time either).

Myth Five: Everything in moderation

Why can't you just eat things in moderation? A square of chocolate here and a salad there. No big deal!

But it *is* a big deal when you and the whole world has been demonizing food for your whole life. It's like the saying "you want what you can't have." You *know* you can have as much celery and dust as your heart desires, but you don't know the same is true for "bad" foods. And that's why we want to eat these so called "bad" foods. They are in limited supply, they are a treat, we mustn't eat too much or the worst thing in the world could happen...we could get fat, oh the horror!

Imagine this: your favourite "bad" food is chocolate. You wake up one morning and find your kitchen cupboards filled to the brim with chocolate, all types, all your favourites and ones you've never tried before. You open the fridge and that too is filled with delicious chocolate cakes, chocolate mousses, chocolate pastries and éclairs. You run the tap in the kitchen and outcomes chocolate milkshake, a never ending supply. Every time you eat a chocolate, it magically re-appears, the supply will *never* dwindle.

You eat chocolate for breakfast, lunch and dinner. In fact, if you *don't* eat chocolate you are insulted and told you should stick to your chocolate diet. But before long, the excitement soon wears off and you begin to start dreading your next meal. You notice that you're craving other foods, but eat chocolate because you "should". You would do anything for a fresh crisp salad right about now, but you're a bad person if you eat a salad, so you sneak it. You go to the salad bar and get a massive bowl, filled with sinful tomatoes, crunchy carrots and cool cucumbers. You eat it quickly, hide the evidence and feel guilty. Tomorrow you'll be extra good and eat more chocolate to make up for being "naughty," slipping with your chocolate diet at the salad bar.

This may seem ridiculous, but this is exactly what we are doing to ourselves by denying ourselves certain foods. If only we knew that we had limitless supplies of chocolate *and* salad *and* any kind of food in the world, it wouldn't be so taboo to us. We wouldn't desire it so badly, we wouldn't dream about it, and fantasize about when we will be reunited with it again.

So, first step to getting off the diet roller coaster of hell, you must realize:

- It's okay to be fat.
- 95% of diets fail.
- Your body will overpower your willpower.
- Food choices are not moral choices.
- Moderation only comes with food freedom.

So how to get off the diet roller coaster? Eat all of the food. Everything. I'm serious. Listen to your body. When you have a craving then follow it. Welcome it, it is your body telling you what you need to focus on/what it needs/what you need to work on. Don't deny yourself. If you hear yourself say "Oh I mustn't" or "I shouldn't eat the whole thing," then let yourself eat it, eat all of it and more.

Now, you may be thinking, "If I let myself eat anything I want, then I will eat forever and then will be so fat and will be totally out of control." Think back to those cupboards of chocolate, the never ending supply. Do you think that you would eventually get bored of never ending chocolate? Yes, you will, but *only* if you fully allow yourself all of the chocolate, not just one or two bars, and *without guilt*. You may think you're wildly greedy. You may be embarrassed, but you must fill your cart at the store with anything your heart desires.

You may be scared that you're going to put on weight. This is a normal and totally expected fear. The reason you are scared of weighing more is because you are suffering from fatphobia. Don't feel bad, most people are fatphobic. Just recognise that, and try to work on the bias you have about being bigger. Also, you may secretly wish that intuitive eating will make you smaller (as it's misinterpreted and sold as a diet by some), and feel a little giddy at the prospect. Fatphobia again! Recognise it again and work on that bias.

Once you feel secure in the knowledge that all food you love has a never ending supply you will start to desire it less. Your tastes will change. You will begin to crave different types of food. You may even find yourself not desiring any food, as all foods are neutral to you. Nothing tickles your fancy. Eventually, you will learn to trust your body when it tells you it's hungry. Your body will begin to trust you too. Your body will no longer need to get you fixated on the foods it did before, as it knows that you won't ever put it back on that horrible roller coaster ever again.

You may go through a period of grieving food. It's kinda sad to lose that thing that used to bring you such tremendous joy. One day, you'll eat that thing you used to love and desire so frantically and just think "meh." Mourn food. It's okay to feel sad that it doesn't bring you the same highs as before. Remember, it doesn't give you the same lows either. You'll feel neutral around food, relaxed. You'll leave stuff on your plate and not be bothered at all. You may forget to eat at times because you're busy.

You'll enjoy food without guilt. You'll eat to nourish yourself and for pleasure at times. Sometimes you'll eat too much, but it won't be a big deal. You won't have rules around food and may even forget what it was like to ride on the diet roller coaster.

At some stage you'll recognise when you're hungry and won't try and suppress that feeling by drinking water to fill your stomach, eating dust cakes or doing something to distract yourself from the ache you feel.

When you eat food and start to feel full you will notice the sensation and without shame or anxiety decide to eat more just for pleasure or leave the rest on your plate.

All of it just won't be that much of a big deal.

I know some of these things sound unbelievable. I know when I learnt about food neutrality I was like "Yeah, right, I can't not eat everything on my plate, people who do that are 100% certified weirdos." It will take time though and it will be difficult. It could be years before you *really* feel neutral around food. It's a journey with ups, downs and windy roads. Also, it's totally ok to use food as comfort. Feeling sad/bored/lonely and want a donut? Eat the donut or 20, it's not a big deal, really. Food is a wonderful thing and can provide us sustenance for our bodies AND our brains.

You will have to talk to those around you and tell them what you're doing so they can support you.

You may have to avoid people who use food shaming language as you will be vulnerable for a while.

You may put on weight, but you will need to examine your own fear or distress about this.

You may lose weight and have to examine your happiness around this fact.

But the good news is that you now know that the roller coaster you're riding on is totally fucked, totally useless, totally damaging to your mental and physical health. Now you just have to slowly get off it, find your footing, and begin to show your body that you truly love and trust it. News Flash: *"Obese," "overweight" and "normal" are categories within the Body Mass Index scale, which is scientifically unsound and total fucking bullshit.

CHAPTER EIGHT:

FIGHT FATPHOBIA

Speaking of fatphobia, let's talk about how that affects everybody, no matter their weight.

I used to be suuuper fatphobic. Like, damn. I would look at other fat people and think things like "Ugh, look at her. She clearly eats so much food! Have some self-control!" or "If only he exercised more, then he wouldn't be so unhealthy! How embarrassing for him." I was fat and still loved judging other fat people, and in turn, myself.

I was suffering from internalised-fatphobia.

What about you? Do you secretly hope that you'll lose weight and dread the idea that loving yourself will lead to permanent weight gain? That's fatphobia. Have you ever seen a super fat person and made judgments about their lifestyle, eating habits or self-respect levels? Fatphobia again. To discriminate against fat people can easily be seen as "acceptable." Of course it's not *actually* acceptable, but your friends likely won't be offended if you suggest that lady over there should really lay off the donuts. Fat people "deserve" this treatment...it's for their own good after all (major eye roll).

A preference for thin is so well established in our culture that it is incredibly difficult to untangle deeply rooted negative beliefs about fat. Your own subconscious biases may be, at times, almost impossible to spot. There are various studies to show that fat people face discrimination at every place in life, making less money than their thin counterparts, not being selected for jobs, being prescribed weight loss for any ailment they present to their doctors (54% of doctors reported that they believe physicians should have the right to withhold treatment from "overweight" or "obese" patients), to name just a few.

Fatphobia literally kills fat people.

You may be horrified by these realities, and you should be, but you may think that being fat (or more fat) yourself is something you just don't want. But why? Because you've been taught to think that fat is bad. And that is fatphobia, my friend.

When we are truly liberated from society's overwhelming beauty ideals, then we would seriously not care what we weighed. We would not stress out if a pair of jeans are too tight. We would not be embarrassed to be seen with a super-sized friend. We would not praise weight loss when someone posts a before and after selfie on Facebook. Instead, we would see the benefits of being fat, like softness, strength and body diversity. We would realize that 67% of women are size 14 or higher and that we are great just the way we are.

If you don't feel like this, then you should challenge these negative biases when they come up. Why do you want to be thin, or thinner? Who defines what is beautiful? Who has the right to decide what weight you should be? Whose fault is it that none of the clothes in the mall fit, when most women are fat?

When you hear biased comments about fat people, speak up.

Don't laugh at fat jokes made by people who are "punching down."

Eat the ice cream if you're afraid it'll make you fat.

Date a fat person.

Watch shows and movies that feature fat people in a positive light (the female led Ghostbusters is ace as is the movie Patty Cake$!).

Hire fat people.

Refuse to talk about diets, cleanses or meal programs.

Include anti-weight discrimination policies in your workplace.

Share images of fat people looking fabulous on social media.

Use the word fat as a neutral descriptor of body types.

Don't praise people for being on diets or losing weight.

And stop that voice in your head in its tracks when it says "You're getting fat" and respond "Yes, and don't I look fabulous, darling."

CHAPTER NINE:

AUDIT YOUR LIFE

A massive part of the process of feeling like a Confidence Warrior for me was finding images of fatties online and getting rid all the diet talk and negativity from my social media feed. The next level to this process is something I call The Life Audit.

The Life Audit is something that I will get my clients to do at the very beginning of their journey to Badassville. The idea is that you look at your life as a whole and notice what things/people/habits etc. make you feel good and get more of that in your life and then notice what makes you feel bad, and get rid of that shit.

There are five areas within our lives to look at:

1. Social media.
2. Friends and family.
3. Patterns and habits.
4. Closet and home.
5. Activities and social gatherings.

Social media we have covered; find images of diverse people, follow folks who look like you, search out images of people who covet parts of their body that you hate on yours. For example, hate your saggy boobs? Follow the #saggyboobsmatter hashtag. There are so many people out there embracing unique and glorious things about themselves, I bet you could find someone who loves what you hate about yourself.

Also, don't forget, get rid of everything and everyone that make you feel less than. It could mean just "unfollowing" someone versus "unfriending" them. Or putting a pause on seeing them in your newsfeed for a while. Whatever works best for you.

Family and friends are the next area. And hoo-boy, is this a tough area to tackle. I used to have friends that I secretly hated. Instead of confronting them or removing them from my life, I would just gossip behind their back. I was not a good friend. I wasn't a good friend because I had low self-esteem and didn't have the courage to have tough conversations. Anyone who was emotionally intelligent would have avoided being friends with me. Present Victoria would never be friends with past Victoria; she was so negative.

Think of the people you spend the most time with. Do you leave your interactions feeling buoyed, with higher energy, inspired, happy, calm? Or do you leave feeling annoyed, frustrated, cross, doubting your greatness? If you're spending time with negative people, then there is no room for new, positive people to come into your life. In this situation you can do a few things, and neither is right or wrong; you'll know what's best for you. One: you could end the relationship, deciding that it's best this person is no longer in your life. This is hard and hopefully, you'll be able to have an honest conversation with the person versus ghosting them. Two: you could try to work on the relationship. Have an honest conversation with them and hope they want the same things as you. Set boundaries with them. This too is hard. It's scary to be open and honest and you don't know how they'll react.

There is a third option: do nothing, say nothing, keep them in your life just as normal and be secretly seething every time you think of them. I don't recommend this option. But you may not be ready to do the difficult work yet, and that's okay. Just know, if you really want to begin to feel great about yourself, then this is a very important step.

The first time you have an honest conversation with someone or gently exit their life, it can feel terrifying, like the scariest thing, like you're a bad person, like you should just be happy with this friend. I know it did for me. But let me tell you, it felt so good *afterwards*.

As I continue to expand and make new friends, I will occasionally come across people from time to time where it's just not a match and I have to "break up" with them. I gotta be honest, I don't find this process easy or fun, but a necessary step in my quest for awesomeness. It is a lot smoother now and takes less time for me to act. Now, I have incredible friends in my life, I truly value them and vice versa. I am actually a good friend now, as I don't secretly hate them! Fancy that, friends that I like? How weird!

So, friends are one thing, but what about family? Queue dramatic music!

This is next level stuff as society tells us that we should always put up with family no matter what, blood is thicker than water and all that. I say that we shouldn't. We shouldn't put up with bad behaviour just because we happen to share a parent, or another relative. Nuh-uh! You can take the same steps as I prescribed with friends, but there is another option. The other option is to reduce the time you are exposed to that family member. Families can be hella complicated and breaking off a relationship with one person could cause lots of consequences that you don't want to deal with right now. And that's okay.

For example, you go around to your parents' house every weekend, and when you leave you are in such a bad mood. Your mom nags you about your life, hinting that you're a disappointment and your dad is super sexist and comments on your weight. How about going over for less time, or only once every other weekend? See how that feels, work out if it's having an impact on how you're feeling about yourself. Another thing you could try is to set firm boundaries. Explain "Hey, I am working on my confidence right now. I've realized that when you talk about my weight it makes me feel less confident. Could you help me out and try not to mention it to me?" If the offender truly cares about your happiness, he or she will try to abide by your request. But, naturally they will probably slip up. When they do, gently remind them. If they slip up again tell them, you will have to leave if they keep talking about your weight (or whatever else you told them to keep to themselves). If they do it a third time, leave.

You may be accused of being very sensitive or overreacting. You are not, your mental health is so incredibly important and these people are not respecting your clearly communicated wishes. Remind them you will only spend time with them if they can refrain from the negative talk, and stick to your guns. This is going to be hard. After years of the same behaviour, it'll be difficult for both parties to change, but it *is* possible. I know, I did it with some of my family members. Still, from time to time I have to correct folks when they make a comment, but we will get there eventually.

Now, what if your family doesn't respect your wishes? What if they continually put you down, make you feel like a big bag of dog poo? You have the option of cutting them from your life, either temporarily or permanently. I have done this too, with a close family member, and as you expect it's not easy. It's hard to avoid one person in your family if you see everyone together. It *can* be done however.

Remember, your mental health is so fucking important. It's not your duty to hurt yourself to maintain a relationship with someone who happened to be born in the same family as you. This will be an ongoing process and you'll notice how some relationships feel great now and may change, and some relationships don't feel great and can change as well. Be gentle with yourself during this process as it's hard and can be all kinds of painful. But remember, growth doesn't happen in a state of comfort.

Next, let's look at patterns and habits. What do you continually *do* that makes your brain sad? What have you slipped into that you detest? Do you say yes to things that really you wanted to say no to, but you felt guilty, or wanted people to like you? An example of a pattern is that you've slowly got into the habit of sleeping in, juuuuust a little bit later every morning. You're not late for work, but you're pretty close. You used to make yourself a nice breakfast and sat with a coffee, but now you're frantically grabbing a coffee to go and going hungry.

Maybe you like doing your hair in the morning and putting on makeup, but your sleeping in habit means that you do this less, and in turn don't feel as nice about yourself when you get to work. Maybe you used to meditate every morning, but going to bed late after going into a YouTube black hole until 2am (me, watching hours of Dr Pimple Popper videos) has taken over your routine and you feel way less calm and relaxed everyday.

So have a think: are there patterns that ultimately make you less happy? Make you feel less worthy. Sleeping in late is just an example. It could be that sleeping in makes you feel like a goddess, and if that's the case keep on keeping on! Habits you may have could include things like agreeing to stay late at work, because you don't want your boss to think you're lazy, when actually you have things planned. It could be overlooking a friend's chronic tardiness, and not saying anything when she shows up 20 minutes late for your lunch date. Or maybe you're the one who always cooks, your partner gets in from work later than you and you just do it, even though you don't like it and feel resentful.

Do you have a habit of being a pushover, a people pleaser, a "I hate you so much" attitude in your brain, but nice to their face tendency? Wanna change that? You can. Start saying no, start telling people how you feel. Start realising that your time is important and so is your mental wellbeing.

Now, time to look at your closet and your home. The things you have in your life. Something we look in everyday reminds us of how we don't measure up: our closet. If you have clothes that no longer fit, or "goal clothes" for when you lose weight taking up space in your bedroom, then you may as well be hanging a sign up that you see everyday reading "You're too big/unworthy/ugly/lazy." Seriously. Think about the neural pathways you're creating! Get rid of that shit! Give them to a new home, store them away, put them in the garbage, DIY them into a new bed for your dog, use them as bonfire kindling. Whatever you do, get them out of your life and out of your sight. That dress you wore to your prom 17 years ago when you were basically still a child will never fit again, and isn't in style and no, no one else wants to wear it either. Want to keep it as a memento? Look at the damn picture of you wearing it at a time you did like it and it fit. Get rid of it.

You'll also be creating space for more things that actually make you feel good. Imagine opening up your wardrobe and seeing gorgeous sequins, or well tailored suits, or dope sportswear and knowing they all fit you and you feel fierce while wearing them. Once you've had fun decluttering your clothes, then look around your house. Do you have things laying around that say "Girl, you're such a loser!"

A giant reminder of your self appointed loserness is your set of scales. Just seeing scales in someone's home gives me the heebie jeebies. How can one tiny piece of metal and glass so quickly define our worth? How much disappointment, shame, frustration, sadness and sometimes joy has this small piece of torture equipment given us?

And what does it really measure? Our gravitational pull to the earth. That's it. Nothing else. It doesn't measure how healthy you are. It doesn't measure if you're a good person, a kind friend. It doesn't measure the amount of love you're capable of giving to others, the capacity of your heart.

So why do we put so much weight into what it tells us (pun intended)?

You need to get rid of that shit from your life. If you're not sure how serious I am about this I will

now spell it out in capital letters for you. GET
RID OF YOUR GODDAMN, MOTHER FUCKING,
PIECE OF SHIT SCALE!

See, very serious, capital letters *and* swearing.

What else do you have that measures your worth
and makes you feel like a big bag of dicks? You may
not even realise something you're using to measure
yourself makes you feel bad until you really think
about it. Do you have a fitbit? A step tracking
device? Do you guilty if you do less steps than you
"should" or that you'd like to? Yup, another piece
of shit measuring device that needs to be gifted to
someone you really hate.

Any other measuring devices lurking whispering
to your subconscious about what a lazy, useless,
waste of space you are? Smash them! Burn them!
Launch them into deep outer space! Bury them six
feet under! Sink them to the bottom of the Mariana
Trench! Go to university to become a scientist
and dedicate your life to learning the solution to
shrink things and then shrink the thing so that only
Borrowers can use these evil items!

These items are the obvious things to boot when it comes to destroying your self esteem, but what about the things in your life that aren't so obvious?

I used to play the piano, it was fun. I eventually lost interest, however, but I didn't want to give away my gorgeous piano keyboard. You know, just in case. So for years I made space for it in my house, moved it to new houses with me, and every time I saw it, the damn thing would melodically whisper, "Oh you used to be *so talented*, now look at you, a failure with no musical ability. What a waste!"

I finally realized after dusting it one day for the millionth time that I need this object out of my life. I sold it online to a teenager who was super excited to have it. I then had extra space to put in a desk to work from home. The piano took up space in my home and in my mind as well. Maybe it stopped me from working on my business as much since I didn't have a dedicated space to work? Maybe it stopped me making more money? Maybe it made me believe I was super lazy? All this from a simple object.

And imagine if you have multiple things like that in your home. How many messages every day you could be getting from them telling you mean things? It could also be objects that are neutral. Something that you barely notice, it's just there and always has been. Perhaps if you got rid of it you'd replace it with something that has a positive influence on you. Maybe a little picture frame with a positive affirmation in it. Have a think about the things that are broken or annoying in some way, but you never get round to fixing them. Everyday when you interact with these things you're getting a shot of "I'm not worth having something that's in working order. I am not worthy." Say your car has a cracked windscreen and this really makes you feel bad. But months go by and you haven't fixed it. Fix the damn thing! It's not about the glass, it's about how it makes you *feel*.

Finally let's look at activities and social gatherings.

Think about all the things you *do* in a day. Probably your biggest activity is going to work. As I mentioned before I always presumed everybody hated their job. Not only hated, but deeply despised it. I used to wait outside one job in particular until the *exact* second I had to go in. I had timed how long it took me to get to the second floor, to my desk and to log into my computer. I couldn't bear spending a single extra second in the building. I thought this was normal. We spend 2080 hours a year at work. What do you think 2080 hours of negativity a year does to our brains? And it's not only time in work, but it's the time you spend dreading it before you go in. There used to be a time on Sunday evening where it went from the weekend to getting ready for the work week that I would stress me out in a massive way.

The jobs I had before I loved myself messed with my mind in an incredible way, and they kept me paralyzed with fear about leaving. I hated my job, but didn't think I was worthy of something better. It was a terrible pattern to be in. The thing I now know is that you just *decide* what you want, and then try to get there. Most people just don't believe they can do that thing they want and so never make it happen. They resign themselves to jobs that make them sad and that's them, forever. The difference between them and the people who "get out" is perception. Perception of worth. Remember

I told you about my boss who wouldn't give me a pay raise? If I was still deep in my low self esteem days, I would've just agreed with him and probably have been traumatized from the experience of him saying no. I may have never asked for another raise and would've felt grateful for the job seeing as I was such a crappy employee.

I was in corporate recruitment for almost nine years and that's what led me into helping people with confidence. I would see time and time again wonderfully talented accomplished, hard working, gregarious job candidates undervalue themselves, and most of the time, these were women. They would question whether they were really a good fit for the job I would put them forward for and ask for the lower range of the salary bracket. Generally speaking, it was the guys who were like "I'm worth a million bucks, baby!" and didn't have the experience to back it up. The thing is these guys would get the job, just because they believed they were worthy.

So if you hate your job, what do you want to do? What do you like in life? What are you good at? What are you passionate about?

Come up with a plan of how to get there. Take small steps. Take leaps. Do research. Get educated on your value in the market. If you are a woman, ask for more than you think you're worth, because you are worth more than you think you are. If you are a woman of color/non binary/trans/ differently abled ask even more than that, because you're already being paid less than you should be. Work on your fear because I promise you with *any* personal growth is fear. No fear - no growth. Believe in yourself, know that it *is* possible to have a job and like it, to LOVE it even. I adore my job and sometimes I think "I can't wait to get sucked into work today!"

Work is probably your biggest activity to tackle. But what about the other things you do? A big one for me was movement for the sake of punishing my bad fat body. I would go to the gym, which I found deathly boring. I would go running, which was so punishing for me and again a total snoozefest. I truly believed that the only "good" exercise was the stuff where you burnt the most calories and hurt your body the most.

Now I do things I actually like! Weird hey. I move my body for fun, not for punishment. I don't push myself to the point where I think I'm going to vomit. I don't workout so I am "allowed" to eat certain foods. I go dancing, and I don't care that I look like a twat. I ride my bike with my dog in the basket and prefer going down hills than up them. I go for walks to nice places and don't make sure to maintain a slow jog because what's the point unless you're out of breath. If I don't want to exercise, I won't. I may want to move my body three times a week, or maybe three times a year. Whatever brings you joy, then do that.

I discovered what activities I actually liked by trying them. If afterwards I was like "nope", then I didn't go again, or tried a different version or instructor. It could be that the movement you like is something simple that you don't count as exercise. For example walking your dog. Movement doesn't always have to be rollerblading on the seawall in neon lycra with a fanny pack for it to be joy inducing or brain stimulating.

So that is the Life Audit, my friend.

A lot of areas to cover, literally your whole life. Ha. There could be areas that don't fall into any one of these five categories. Just notice what you're doing during your day and take stock of how it makes you *feel*.

Your feelings are real and valid and you deserve to live a life that makes you inspired, confident, a life that makes you feel like a #FierceFatty!

CHAPTER TEN:

CONCLUSION

So, is my life perfect now that I've stopped dieting and love my body? In a word: no. But fuck me, my life is SO much better! I have stopped wasting precious mindspace on the unhelpful and unrealistic thought that being thin would mean happiness, fulfillment and love. I now have the mental energy to pursue things in life that make me happy, because I don't have a constant, ever present monologue from my inner critic running through my mind telling me that I am a horrible hag and shouldn't be seen in public. I have done things that young Victoria could not even fathom as possible because of this.

I have better relationships now. My mom and I talk about the things that happened in the past, and I can say with confidence that we have both changed as people. My mom's love for me cannot be measured, and anything she did in the past that hurt me brings her tremendous pain.

I was even able to come to a place of understanding and peace with my dad. He also had changed, saying he vowed to be a wonderful grandfather seeing as he was such a bad dad, and he got to do that for six months before he died suddenly. There was a delivery left on his doorstep after his death, that was yet another present purchased for his grandson, that he never got to give him.

There are days however when a negative thought will flash through my head. My dad was discovered dead a week before my TEDx talk. I was under extreme stress. I got a stomach bug a few days after his funeral and because of that I lost a little weight. Looking in the mirror at the minor changes in my body a thought came to me; "now you'll get more dates because you're thinner, the boys are gonna really like you now." That thought came to me because it was a tough time for me. The difference now is that I realise that the thought is totally bogus and flashed through my head because I was in a weakened state. Before I could have embarked on another diet to try and get some control in my life, but this time around I just embarked on some serious self care.

Now I am resilient, and I want that for you if you're not there yet. Nothing is ever going to be perfect, but if we get ready for battle arming ourselves with knowledge and join the fight together we can become Confidence Warriors and Fierce Fatties.

There is an army of us out there already and we are only getting stronger and more numerous every day.

I was *so* wrong when I believed that thin equaled happy and healthy, and that fat equaled unhappy and unhealthy. If you take one thing from this book, let it be that fact.

No matter what negative beliefs you are holding onto, you can flip the script and find joy in something that used to bring you shame. YOU can be a rebel.

Love your fabulous body, unconditionally. Ditch toxic influences and choose positive friends.

What if we shifted focus, and stopped being so damn scared of fatness? Then maybe people would be valued not by the number that displays on the scale but on the capacity of their hearts. Our minds could be free to explore our true passions instead of being consumed by how many pieces of super sinful, zero fat, no sugar, paleo chocolate we have eaten that day. We could see the blessing of having diverse body types in our culture. We could see the benefits of being fat, like increased buoyancy in water. The best hugs come from fat people!

Take your body on adventures. Do the things that truly make you happy. Whether your bum jiggles while you do it or not.

Don't listen to your inner critic when it's being a jerk. Realize that average person walking past you on the street is not thinking how hideous and disgusting you are, but are probably wrapped up in their own thoughts and insecurities, hoping that people like them, that people love them...just like you.

So, what if you truly believed that "You are worthy, you always were, and you always will be?" Who knows, maybe you'd win gold at the Olympics, be the next 80 year old woman to invent Tinder for seniors. Or maybe, you'd be that one whale who dared to dance in a bikini. Like I did on stage, in front of 2600 people.

#FierceFatties unite!

Credit: Len Grinke

WORK WITH ME

Did you love this book and want some more BAM POW LIFE awesomeness in your brain? Want to really work on becoming a Fierce Fatty? Terrific!

Why not sign up for my free 10 day eCourse Extreme Confidence Makeover at www.bampowlife.com/extremeconfidencemakeover

Or perhaps you want to be surrounded by other Fierce Fatties? Then you can join my membership club, Confidence Warrior Club. I have free and pro levels of membership. Go to www.bampowlife.com/confidencewarriorclub

My flagship eCourse, Fierce Fatty, is available sporadically throughout the year and so make sure to join the waitlist to hear when it is next available at www.fiercefatty.com

STUDY OF CANADIANS ON FAT BIAS: COMPLETE RESULTS

What is your ideal body shape?

Athletic: 29.5%

Average: 29.1%

Curvy: 23.3%

Thin: 10.0%

Fat: 8.1%

What is your least desired body shape?

Fat: 56.2%

Thin: 21.7%

Athletic: 11.9%

Average: 8.9%

Curvy: 1.3%

Do you think people should love their bodies?

Yes: 73.1%

Maybe: 17.6%

No: 9.2%

Do you think fat people should love their bodies?

Yes: 54.4%

Only if they're "healthy": 32.6%

No: 13.1%

What word would you use to describe a fat person?

Unhealthy: 36.2%

Average: 21.0%

Cuddly: 13.9%

Undisciplined: 7.9%

What word would you use to describe an "average" sized person?

Healthy: 40.6%

In control: 34.7%

Fit: 10.8%

Boring: 7.7%

What would be worse? Being fat or:

Losing your job tomorrow: 100% being fat is worse

Having the flu for a month: 100% being fat is worse

Have people think you're a bad person: 90% being fat is worse

Be publically humiliated: 90% being fat is worse

Not be able to do your favourite hobby: 100% being fat is worse

Work with your archenemy for the rest of your career: 100% being fat is worse

Get cheated on by the spouse you adore: 100% being fat is worse

AUTHOR BIOGRAPHY

Victoria Welsby is a body image activist, confidence expert, Adjunct Professor at the University of British Columbia and TEDx speaker. She went from being homeless, abused with self-esteem that was achingly low into the courageous fat activist and change maker she is today. Victoria helps people fall in love with themselves and is dedicated to modifying the way society views fat bodies.

Links:

Website: www.bampowlife.com
Instagram: @bampowlife
Facebook: @bampowlife
Twitter: @bampowlife
Pinterest: @bampowlife
YouTube: @bampowlife
LinkedIn: @victoriawelsby
Email: victoria@bampowlife.com

Made in the USA
Monee, IL
07 September 2020